Thrills and Chills
Roller Coaste

Written by Jeff Savage

Contents

Roller Coasters Over Time 2

Types of Roller Coasters 4

Designing High-Tech Thrills 6

Roller Coaster Safety 9

Favorite Roller Coasters 10

Glossary 12

PEARSON

Roller Coasters Over Time

Do you consider yourself a thrill seeker? If so, then climb aboard the Desperado at Buffalo Bill's in Nevada and hang on tight. This hair-raising roller coaster begins inside a hotel lobby. Riders hold on tight as it gradually ascends the 209-foot-high lift hill. It then plunges 225 feet and bursts through an underground tunnel at speeds of up to 80 miles per hour (mph). Guests in the hotel lobby can't believe their eyes as they observe the coaster race through the tunnel. As the coaster comes to a halt, riders quickly climb out of the cars and can't wait to experience the thrills and chills all over again.

Roller coasters originated in fifteenth-century Russia, where townspeople built large ice slides out of wood, some as high as 70 feet. Riders slid down on blocks of ice shaped like sleds, with seats lined with straw for warmth and comfort. Sand was used to slow down the frozen sleds once they reached the bottom of the ride. Riders had to walk back to the top for another turn on the frozen sleds. Over time, cars with small wheels replaced the sleds, eliminating the need for ice. Eventually, a continuous track and a cable were added to lift the car upward to its starting position.✱ These coasters moved at speeds of up to 50 mph and often jumped off the tracks.

On June 13, 1884, America's first roller coaster, designed by an inventor from Ohio, opened at Coney Island in Brooklyn, New York. The ride was built on wooden tracks and admission was just five cents. Riders started at a height of 50 feet and rode for more than 600 feet at 6 mph. After the last dip, they got off the train as it switched to another track to return up the hill. Soon, wooden coasters were at amusement parks everywhere. By the end of the 1920s, there were more than 1,500 roller coasters in the United States.

Roller Coaster Timeline

1400s
Russians enjoy ice slides.

1884
America's first roller coaster opens at Coney Island.

1959
Disney builds the first tubular-steel roller coaster.

1992
Six Flags America is home to the first successful inverted coaster.

1994
Desperado is one of the first **hypercoasters**.

Many amusement parks were torn down or abandoned during the Great Depression. In 1930, there were between 1,800 and 2,000 amusement parks in the United States. By 1939, that number had dwindled to 245. It wasn't until after World War II that the number of amusement parks began to increase once more. In 1959, Disneyland® opened the Matterhorn Bobsleds, the world's first tubular-steel coaster. This thrilling coaster ride had a **corkscrew** track with sharper twists and turns for maximum thrills.

Types of Roller Coasters

There are two major types of roller coasters—wooden and steel. Wooden coasters are designed with wooden tracks that usually complete a full **circuit**. Steel coasters are usually a full-circuit ride with steel tracks. Size and speed can be similar for both types of coasters. However, steel coasters tend to offer riders a smoother ride. The ability of steel to stretch enables designers to create taller and faster coasters. Steel structures can be twisted into loops, corkscrews, and sharp **hairpin turns**. They also don't require as much **scaffolding** as wooden coasters need. Some steel coasters operate on a shuttle circuit in which the coaster travels back and forth on the same track.

Wooden Coaster

Steel Coaster

Steel Coaster

5

Designing High-Tech Thrills

Designs of the actual coaster rides vary. There are stand-up coasters, suspended coasters, and lie-down coasters. The Medusa is the first floorless, frontless, and sideless coaster in which riders are secured to a seat by a shoulder harness. Then they are hurtled along the coaster's tracks at speeds of up to 61 mph. Riders on the Batwing are sent through a corkscrew structure while lying on their backs. At some points in the ride, riders hang horizontally below the track facedown.

Every hill, dip, and curve on a roller coaster has been designed to safely scare riders. Designers collaborate to create thrilling rides. New technology helps roller coasters run faster and more smoothly. Computers are used to figure **pitches**, steep slopes, and sharp curves. They evaluate the effects of high speeds on the coaster car and the riders. They also help to judge the effects of force, temperature, and vibration levels. As a result, today there are all kinds of thrill rides that send riders to the edge.

Roller coaster designer Alan Schilke uses his understanding of physics to design thrill rides.

The first roller coasters were powered by gravity. A motor and **pulley** pulled the ride up the first steep hill, and then gravity took over once the ride gained enough speed and energy to make it up the next hill. The first hill was always the tallest to ensure that the coaster had enough energy to make it to the end of the ride.

Engineers have found other ways to make more powerful, yet safe, roller coasters. For some rides, chain pulleys that lift cars at the rate of 5 or 6 feet per second have been replaced with elevator cable systems that climb 20 feet per second. These types of changes increase the number of rides per hour.

Fred Bolingbroke, manufacturer of X, and Alan Schilke pose with the roller coaster that makes riders feel like they are sky diving.

The HyperSonic XLC coaster is launched with **compressed** air. This air-powered coaster uses 400 horsepower to send riders from 0 to 80 mph in under 2 seconds. The use of **electromagnetic waves** to launch a coaster has replaced chain-and-pulley systems in some coasters. A motor developed to launch rockets is the force behind the Mr. Freeze coaster. Its cars have metal fins on the bottom that fit between two tracks of **electromagnets**. High-powered magnets launch the cars like a slingshot, causing the coaster to go from 0 to 70 mph in about 4 seconds.

As of 2005, Kingda Ka, a "rocket" coaster in New Jersey, is the world's tallest and fastest coaster. It launches riders from 0 to 128 mph in 3.5 seconds. A special system of motors called hydraulics makes this speed possible. Riders initially blast off along a flat track, and then the coaster begins climbing 456 feet at a straight 90-degree angle. When the coaster reaches this record-breaking height, it plummets 418 feet straight down on the other side.

Seats on X are paired on either side of the track. They revolve 360 degrees as the coaster twists.

Roller Coaster Safety

Statistically, riding on a roller coaster is safer than riding on a bicycle or in a car. New coasters are tested with bags filled with sand, which are belted into the actual cars. Minimum height, weight, and age restrictions are based on the ride's force. Lap bars and harnesses keep riders safely in their seats. Extra wheels on the cars grip the track from above and below to keep the cars on the track. Inspectors examine the tracks daily to make sure the structure is safe. Above all, engineers use the **laws of physics** to make sure each ride is safe. In some rides, the force of gravity is stronger than what astronauts feel at liftoff!

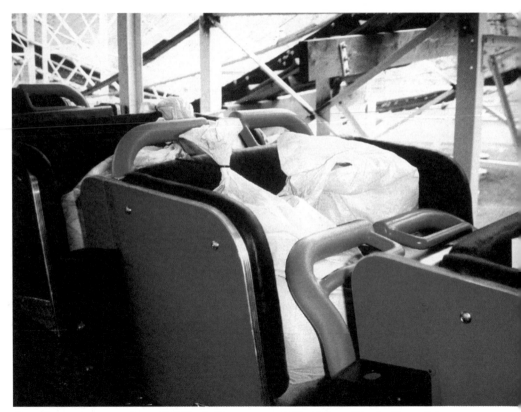

Sandbags are used on Riddler's Revenge at Six Flags Magic Mountain to approximate the weight of passengers as engineers test the ride.

Favorite Roller Coasters

The material used to build a roller coaster track impacts the overall ride and design. The majority of roller coasters in the United States are made of steel. One of the tallest steel roller coasters in North America is Top Thrill Dragster. Right behind it are Superman: The Escape, and Millennium Force. However, some riders still like the designs and rickety sounds of the wooden coaster. One of the tallest and fastest wooden coasters is the Son of Beast. Speeding right behind are two more "woodies"—Boss and American Eagle.

Name	Place	Material	Speed	Height
Kingda Ka	New Jersey	steel	128 mph	456 ft
Top Thrill Dragster	Ohio	steel	120 mph	420 ft
Superman: The Escape	California	steel	100 mph	415 ft
Millennium Force	Ohio	steel	93 mph	310 ft
Desperado	Nevada	steel	80 mph	225 ft
HyperSonic XLC	Virginia	steel	80 mph	165 ft
Son of Beast	Ohio	wood	78.3 mph	218 ft
Mr. Freeze	Texas, Missouri	steel	70 mph	218 ft
Boss	Missouri	wood	66.3 mph	122 ft
American Eagle	Illinois	wood	66 mph	127 ft

Cedar Point is the second-oldest amusement park in the United States. It's home to Millennium Force, one of the tallest coasters in the world.

With ever-advancing technology, the list of the best rides changes yearly. Just when you think you've ridden the tallest, fastest roller coaster in the world, a new one comes along to break the record.

Glossary

circuit   a movement or track that is circular in shape

compressed   squeezed or pressed very tightly

corkscrew   having a twisted or spiral shape

electromagnetic waves   waves of energy that can travel through empty space, such as radio waves and X-rays

electromagnets   magnets that are formed by wrapping pieces of iron in wire and passing electricity through the wire

hairpin turns   sharp, U-shaped turns

hypercoasters   types of roller coasters that are extremely tall and reach very high speeds

laws of physics   conclusions that scientists have made about matter and energy and how it will behave, based on their observations

pitches   steep slants or slopes and their measurement

pulley   a small wheel having a groove in which a rope or belt moves; it is used to lift objects

scaffolding   a raised framework made of wood or metal, used as a support

statistically   using the facts or data in the form of numbers that have been collected about a subject